OTHER BOOKS BY DAVE MORICE

POETRY
POEMS (Privately published by Al Buck)
TILT (Toothpaste Press)
JND-SONG OF THE GOLDEN GRADRTI (The Happy Press)
THE CUTIST ANTHOLOGY (The Happy Press)
QUICKSAND THROUGH THE HOURGLASS (Toothpaste Press)

CHILDREN'S BOOKS
A VISIT FROM ST. ALPHABET (Toothpaste Press)
DOT TOWN (Toothpaste Press)

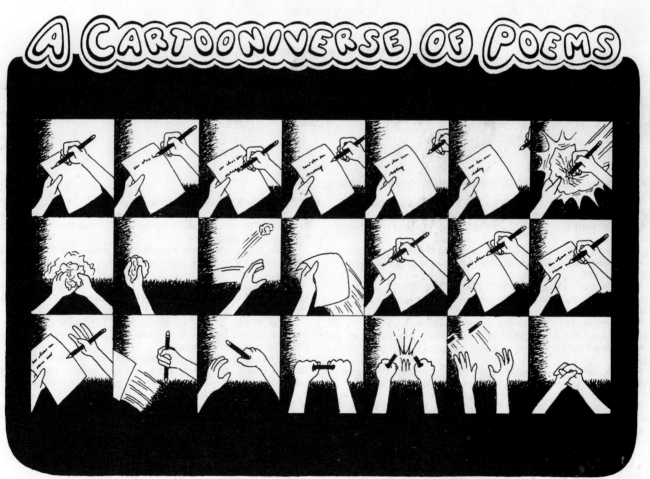

by Dave Morice

Simon and Schuster · New York

1 3 5 7 9 10 8 6 4 2

Library of Congress Cataloging in Publication Data

Morice, Dave, 1946–
Poetry comics.

1. English poetry. 2. American poetry.
3. American wit and humor, Pictorial.
I. Title. II. Title: Cartooniverse of poems.
PR1175.M627   1982   821'.008   82-10590
ISBN 0-671-45486-2
0-671-45972-4 Pbk.

The author gratefully acknowledges permission to reprint the following:

"The Red Wheelbarrow" by William Carlos Williams from *The Collected Earlier Poems of William Carlos Williams*, copyright 1938 by New Directions Publishing Corporation and reprinted with their permission.

"The Songs of Maximus, Song I," copyright © 1960 by Charles Olson. Published by Jargon/Corinth Books and reprinted with their permission.

"Empty Words," copyright © 1974 and 1975 by John Cage. Reprinted from *Empty Words* by permission of Wesleyan University Press.

"The Recollection" by Denise Levertov, reprinted from *The Freeing of the Dust*, copyright © 1975 by Denise Levertov Goodman. Reprinted by permission of New Directions Publishing Corporation.

"A Supermarket in California" and "Howl" by Allen Ginsberg from *Howl and Other Poems*, copyright © 1956, 1959 by Allen Ginsberg. Reprinted by permission of City Lights Books.

"Oh No" by Robert Creeley, reprinted from *For Love: Poems 1950–1960*, copyright © 1962 by Robert Creeley. Reprinted by permission of Charles Scribner's Sons.

"The Corner" by Donald Hall, reprinted from *The Alligator Bride*, copyright © 1969. Published by Harper & Row, Publishers, Inc. Reprinted by permission of Donald Hall.

"Secrets of the Estate" by Tom Clark reprinted from *The End of the Line*, copyright © 1980. Published by Little Caesar Press. Reprinted by permission of Tom Clark.

"Big Ant in Springtime" by David Hilton, reprinted from *The Candleflame*, copyright © 1976. Published by The Toothpaste Press. Reprinted with permission.

"The Poem Machine" by Darrell Gray, reprinted from *Something Swims Out*, copyright © 1971. Published by Blue Wind Press as Search for Tomorrow Special Number A, George Mattingly, Editor. Reprinted with permission.

"Ubble Snop: by Joyce Holland, reprinted from *The Final E*, copyright © 1978. Published by X Press. Reprinted with permission.

"The Pinball Manifesto" by Allan Kornblum, reprinted from *The Salad Bushes*, copyright © 1975, 1980. Published by The Seamark Press and The Toothpaste Press. Reprinted with permission.

"Break, Break, Break" by Alfred, Lord Tennyson, cartoon version copyright © 1981 by D. Morice, published in *Riverrun* magazine. Reprinted with permission.

"The Eagle" by Alfred, Lord Tennyson and "On the Horizon" by Stephen Crane; cartoon versions first appeared in *Rocky Ledge* magazine, number 6, copyright © 1980 by Reed Bye. Reprinted by permission of the editors.

"The Songs of Maximus, Song I"; cartoon version first appeared in *Red Hand Book II*, copyright © 1980 by Pynon Press, Atlanta. Reprinted with permission.

"Howl" by Allen Ginsberg; cartoon version first appeared in New Blood Magazine, copyright © 1981 by New Blood Press. Reprinted with permission.

"Gershwin Headache" by FM Cotolo, copyright © 1981 by FM Cotolo. Cartoon version first published by Fat Tuesday Press, copyright © 1981. Reprinted with permission.

ACKNOWLEDGMENTS

Thanks to the following publications, in which some of the Comics have appeared: Magazines: *Abraxas, Fat Tuesday, Flue, Luna Tack, Iowa Woman, Kite, New Blood, North American Review, Phantasm, Poetry Flash, Red Hand Book, Riverrun, Rocky Ledge, Smoke Signals, Telephone, Turkey Buzzard;* Newspapers: *Baltimore City Paper, Cedar Rapids Gazette, Des Moines Register, St. Louis Mirror;* Postcards: *Hard Press;* Anthologies: *Scenarios, Sparks of Fire.*

Thanks to the following organizations for their help: Coordinating Council of Literary Magazines (CCLM) for the 1981 grant to the magazine *Poetry Comics;* Poets and Writers, Inc.

And many thanks, for many reasons, to: Lauren Klapper, Ralston Bedge, Bobbi Nowland, Stu Mead, Becky Johns, Jeff Weinstein.

FOR
Lil,
Gil,
Delaine,
Craig,
Michele,
Jeannie,
The Sunday Funnies,
and
The Norton Anthology.

CONTENTS

Most of the cartoons in this book contain the entire poem. In some cases (indicated by asterisks* below) the cartoons present excerpts from the original verse.

INTRODUCTION

A few years ago a friend of mine said, "Great poems should paint pictures in the mind." Jokingly, I replied that great poems would make great cartoons, and what began as a wisecrack soon evolved into a diabolical plot to overthrow the Foundations of Poetry. With the gleeful encouragement of other contemporary poets, I cartoonized poem after poem and published them in my magazine, *Poetry Comics,* and in other such literary journals.

My hat goes off to the editors and writers of the small press world. If it weren't for them, *Poetry Comics* wouldn't have been much more than a paper peddled on a street corner in Iowa City.

Now it's in your hands. Quick! Turn the page!

9

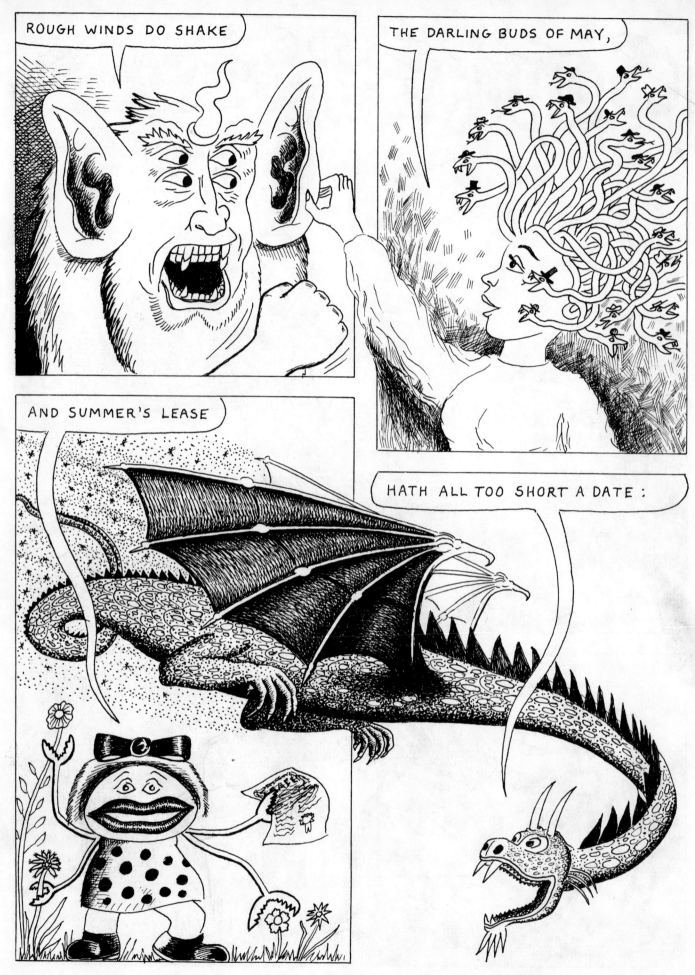

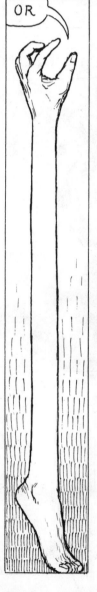

BUT THY ETERNAL SUMMER

SHALL NOT

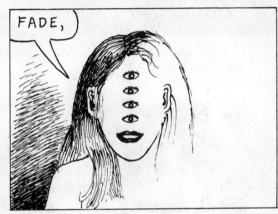

FADE,

NOR LOSE POSSESSION

OF THAT FAIR

THOU OW'ST;

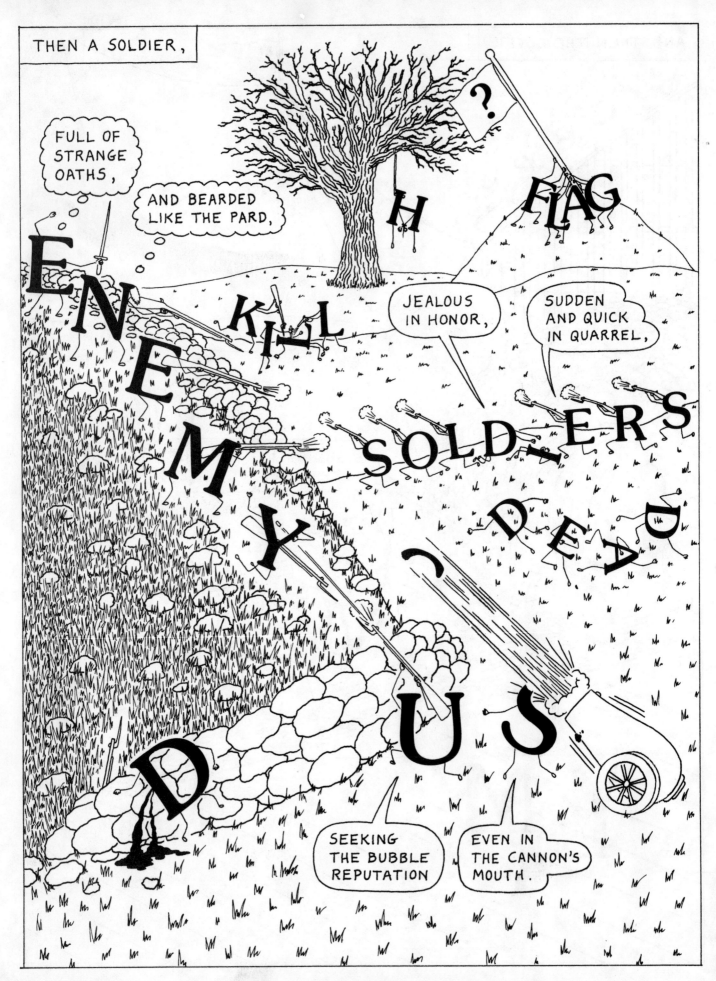

FROM "THE TEMPEST" BY WILLIAM SHAKESPEARE

26

END

"LET ME NOT TO THE MARRIAGE OF TRUE MINDS ADMIT IMPEDIMENTS."

WILLIAM SHAKESPEARE

"THOU HAST MADE ME, AND SHALL THY WORK DECAY?
REPAIR ME NOW, FOR MINE END DOTH HASTE;"

JOHN DONNE

SLOW, SLOW, FRESH FOUN'T

BY BEN JOHNSON

SLOW, SLOW, FRESH FOUNT, KEEP TIME WITH MY SALT TEARS;

YET SLOWER, YET, O FAINTLY, GENTLE SPRINGS!

LIST TO THE HEAVY PART THE MUSIC BEARS,

BOING!
BOING!
BOING!
BOING!

BUT

MIGHT I

OF JOVE'S NECTAR SUP,

I WOULD NOT CHANGE FOR THINE.

I SENT THEE LATE A ROSY WREATH,

NOT SO MUCH HONORING THEE,

END

UPON JULIA'S CLOTHES

BY ROBERT HERRICK

NEXT, WHEN I CAST MINE EYES, AND SEE

THAT BRAVE VIBRATION, EACH WAY FREE,

O, HOW THAT GLITTERING TAKETH ME!

END

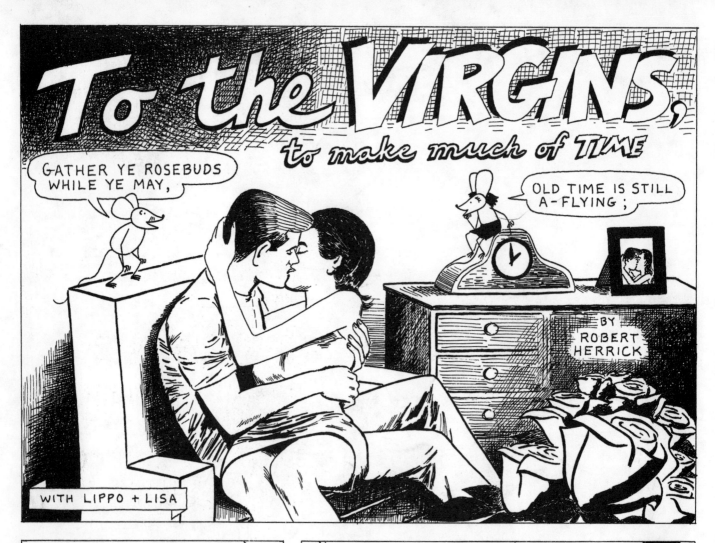

41

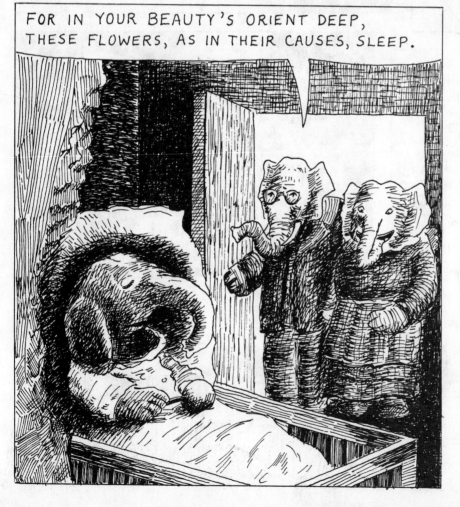

THE GOLDEN ATOMS OF THE DAY·;

FOR IN PURE LOVE HEAVEN DID PREPARE THOSE POWDERS TO ENRICH YOUR HAIR.

ASK ME NO MORE WHITHER DOTH HASTE

THE NIGHTINGALE, WHEN MAY IS PAST;

FOR IN YOUR SWEET DIVIDING THROAT SHE WINTERS, AND KEEPS WARM HER NOTE.

45

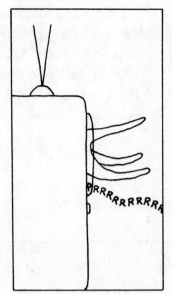

END

My Cat Jeoffry

by Christopher "Kit" Smart

For I will consider
my Cat Jeoffry.

For he is the servant
of the Living God
duly and daily serving him.

For at the first glance
of the glory of God in the East
he worships in his way.

For is this done
by wreathing his body
seven times round
with elegant quickness.

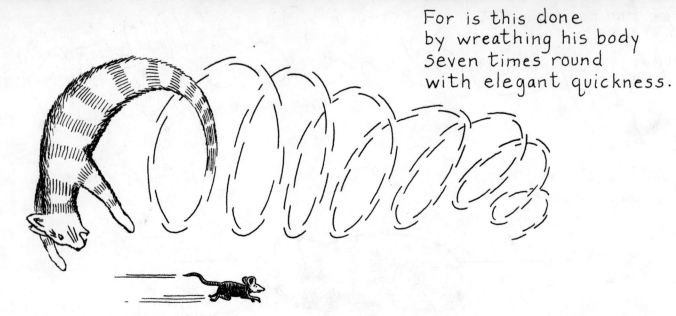

For then he leaps up
to catch the musk,
which is the blessing of God
upon his prayer.

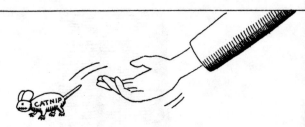

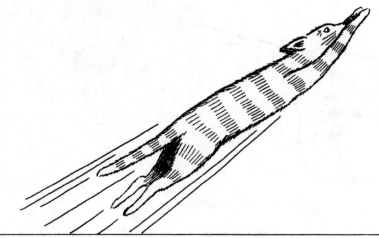

For he rolls
upon prank
to work it in.

For having done duty
and received blessing
he begins to consider
himself.

For this he performs in ten degrees.

For first
he looks upon his fore-paws
to see if they are clean.

For secondly
he kicks up behind
to clear away there.

For thirdly
he works it
upon stretch
with the fore paws
extended.

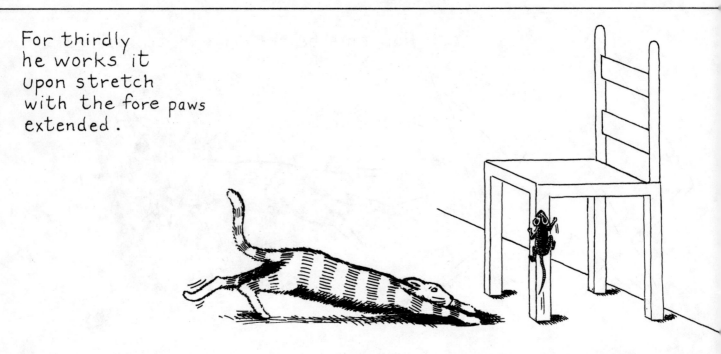

For fourthly
he sharpens his paws
by wood.

54

For fifthly
he washes himself.

For sixthly
he rolls
upon wash.

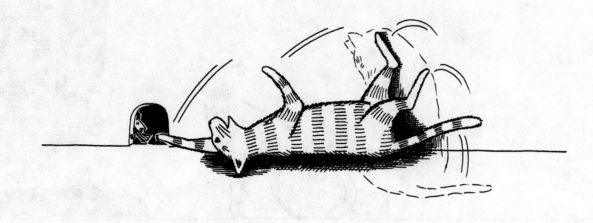

For Seventhly
he fleas himself,
that he may not
be interrupted
upon the beat.

For Eighthly he rubs himself against a post.

For Ninethly he looks up for his instructions.

For Tenthly he goes in quest of food.

For having considered
God and himself
he will consider
his neighbour.

For if he meets
another cat
he will kiss her
in kindness.

For when he takes his prey
he plays with it
to give it a chance.

The End

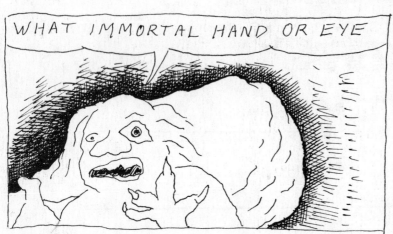

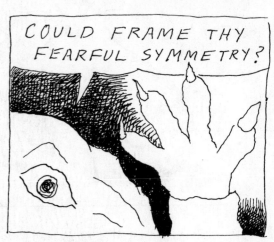

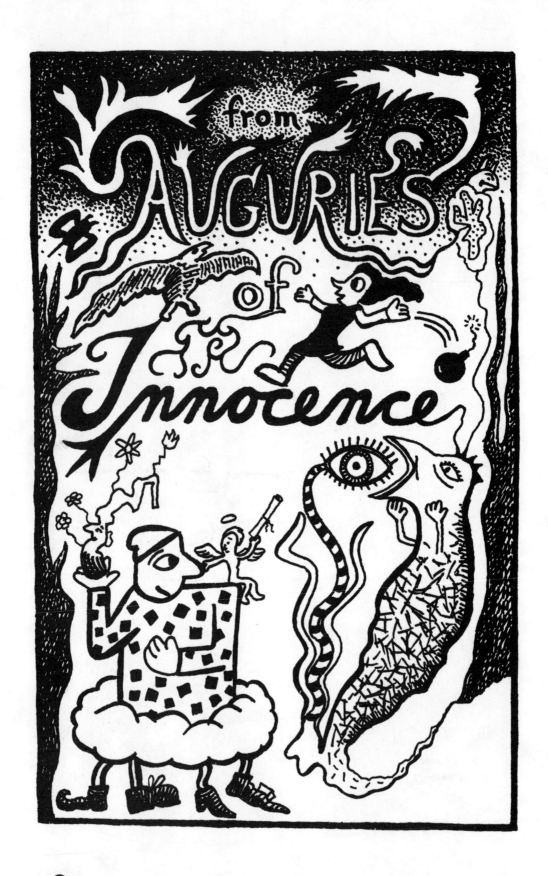

A Poem by William Blake

To see a World in a Grain of Sand

And a Heaven in a Wild flower,

Hold Infinity in the palm of your hand

And Eternity in an hour.

End

IN **XANADU** DID KUBLA KHAN
A STATELY PLEASURE DOME DECREE:

WHERE ALPH, THE SACRED RIVER, RAN

ALPH

THROUGH CAVERNS MEASURELESS TO MAN

DOWN TO A SUNLESS SEA.

SO TWICE FIVE MILES OF

FERTILE GROUND

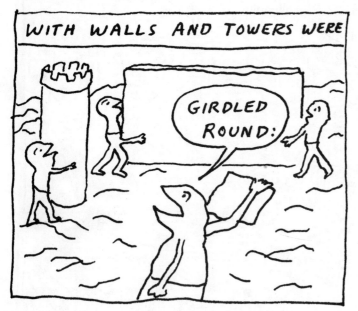

WITH WALLS AND TOWERS WERE

GIRDLED ROUND:

AND THERE WERE GARDENS

BRIGHT

WITH SINUOUS RILLS,

WHERE BLOSSOMED MANY AN

INCENSE-BEARING TREE;

AND HERE WERE FORESTS

ANCIENT AS THE HILLS,

ENFOLDING

SUNNY SPOTS OF GREENERY.

BUT OH! THAT DEEP ROMANTIC CHASM WHICH SLANTED DOWN THE GREEN HILL ATHWART A CEDARN COVER!

A SAVAGE PLACE!

AS HOLY AND ENCHANTED AS E'ER BENEATH THE WANING MOON WAS HAUNTED

BOOOOOOOO

BY WOMAN WAILING

BOOOOOOOO O
HOOOOOOOOO

FOR HER

DEMON LOVER!

FIVE MILES MEANDERING WITH A MAZY*MOTION THROUGH WOOD AND DALE THE SACRED RIVER RAN, THEN REACHED THE CAVERNS MEASURELESS TO MAN, AND SANK IN TUMULT TO A LIFELESS OCEAN:

*(HELP THE TWO LOVERS SWIM TO SAFETY THROUGH THE RIVER TO THE LIFELESS OCEAN BY WORKING THE MAZE!)

LIFELESS OCEAN

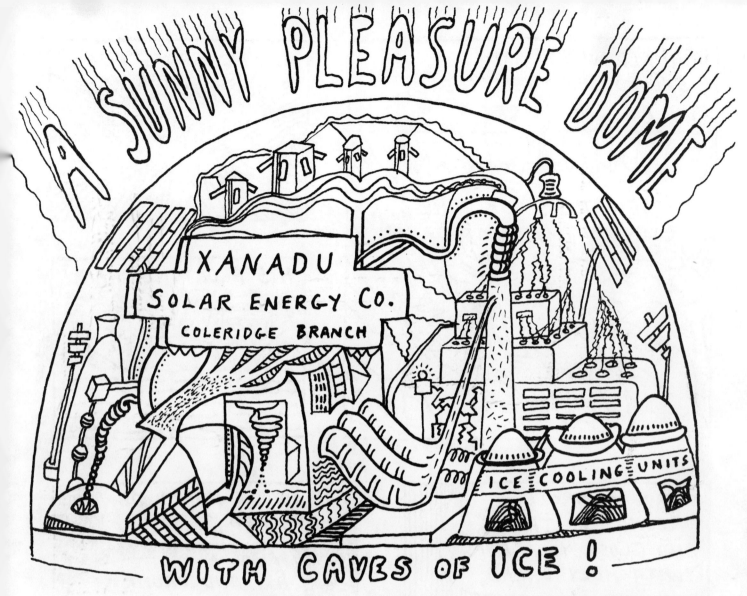

AND ALL WHO HEARD
SHOULD SEE THEM THERE,
AND ALL SHOULD CRY,

BEWARE! BEWARE!

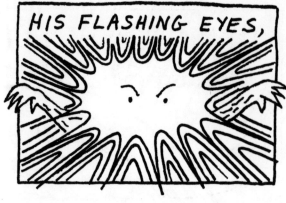

HIS FLASHING EYES,

HIS FLOATING HAIR!

WEAVE A CIRCLE
ROUND HIM THRICE,
AND CLOSE YOUR EYES
WITH HOLY DREAD,

FOR HE ON HONEY DEW
HATH FED,

AND DRUNK
THE MILK
OF PARADISE.

PARADISE DAIRY

END

DYING SPEECH OF AN OLD PHILOSOPHER

BY WALTER SAVAGE LANDOR

I STROVE WITH NONE, FOR NONE WAS WORTH MY STRIFE:

NATURE I LOVED, AND, NEXT TO NATURE, ART:

I WARMED BOTH HANDS BEFORE THE FIRE OF LIFE;

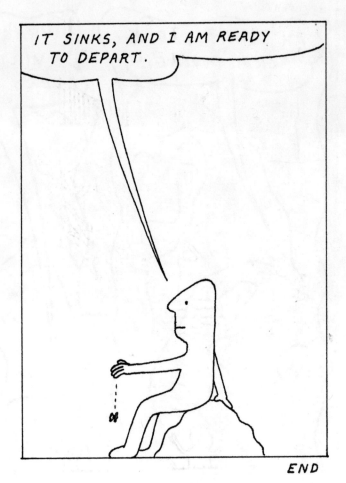

IT SINKS, AND I AM READY TO DEPART.

END

"PAST RUINED ILION HELEN LIVES,"

WALTER SAVAGE LANDOR

"THE KEEN STARS WERE TWINKLING,
AND THE FAIR MOON WAS RISING AMONG THEM,
DEAR JANE ! "

PERCY BYSSHE SHELLEY

TELL THAT ITS SCULPTOR WELL THOSE PASSIONS READ

WHICH YET SURVIVE

STAMPED ON THESE LIFELESS THINGS,

THE HAND THAT MOCKED THEM,

AND THE HEART THAT FED:

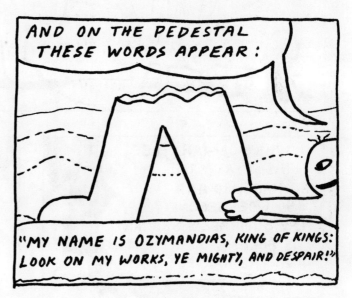

AND ON THE PEDESTAL THESE WORDS APPEAR:

"MY NAME IS OZYMANDIAS, KING OF KINGS: LOOK ON MY WORKS, YE MIGHTY, AND DESPAIR!"

NOTHING BESIDE REMAINS. ROUND THE DECAY OF THAT COLLOSAL WRECK,

BOUNDLESS AND BARE

THE LONE AND LEVEL SANDS STRETCH FAR AWAY.

END

I MET A LADY IN THE MEADS,
FULL BEAUTIFUL — A FAERY'S CHILD,

HER HAIR WAS LONG,
HER FOOT WAS LIGHT,
AND HER EYES WERE WILD.

I MADE A GARLAND
FOR HER HEAD,
AND BRACELETS TOO,
AND FRAGRANT ZONE;

SHE LOOKED AT ME AS SHE DID LOVE,
AND MADE SWEET MOAN.

I SET HER ON MY PACING STEED,
AND NOTHING ELSE SAW ALL DAY LONG,
FOR SIDELONG SHE WOULD BEND, AND SING
A FAERY'S SONG.

SHE FOUND ME ROOTS OF RELISH SWEET, AND HONEY WILD, AND MANNA DEW,

AND SURE IN LANGUAGE STRANGE SHE SAID — "I LOVE THEE TRUE."

SHE TOOK ME TO HER ELFIN GROT, AND THERE SHE WEPT, AND SIGH'D FULL SORE,

ELFIN GROT

AND THERE I SHUT HER WILD, WILD EYES WITH KISSES FOUR.

AND THERE SHE LULLÉD ME TO SLEEP, AND THERE I DREAM'D — AH! WOE BETIDE!

THE LATEST DREAM I EVER DREAM'D ON THE COLD HILL SIDE.

ELFIN GROT

88

END

WHEN I HAVE FEARS

BY JOHN KEATS

DR. BYRON LORD, PSYCHIATRIST

WHEN I HAVE FEARS THAT I MAY CEASE TO BE

BEFORE MY PEN HAS GLEANED MY TEEMING BRAIN,

BEFORE HIGH-PILÉD BOOKS, IN CHARACT'RY, HOLD LIKE RICH GARNERS THE FULL RIPENED GRAIN;

WHEN I BEHOLD, UPON THE NIGHT'S STARRED FACE,

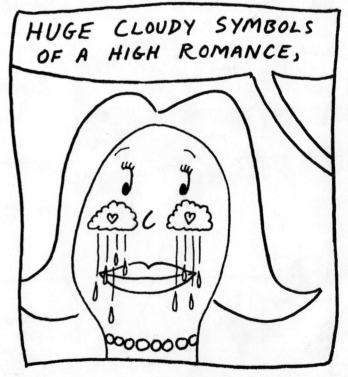

HUGE CLOUDY SYMBOLS OF A HIGH ROMANCE,

This Living Hand

BY JOHN KEATS

THIS LIVING HAND, NOW WARM AND CAPABLE OF EARNEST GRASPING,

WOULD, IF IT WERE COLD AND IN THE ICY SILENCE OF THE TOMB,

SO HAUNT THY DAYS AND CHILL THY DREAMING NIGHTS

THAT THOU WOULDST WISH THINE OWN HEART DRY OF BLOOD

SO IN MY VEINS RED LIFE MIGHT STREAM AGAIN.

AND THOU BE CONSCIENCE-CALMED—

SEE HERE IT IS — I HOLD IT TOWARDS YOU.

END

How Do I Love Thee?

LET ME COUNT THE WAYS.

BY ELIZABETH BARRETT BROWNING

I LOVE THEE TO THE DEPTH AND BREADTH AND HEIGHT

MY SOUL CAN REACH, WHEN

FEELING OUT OF SIGHT

FOR THE ENDS OF BEING AND IDEAL GRACE.

I LOVE THEE TO THE LEVEL OF EVERYDAY'S

MOST QUIET NEED,

BY SUN

AND CANDLE-LIGHT

I LOVE THEE FREELY, AS MEN STRIVE FOR RIGHT;

I LOVE THEE PURELY, AS THEY TURN FROM PRAISE.

I LOVE THEE WITH A PASSION PUT TO USE

IN MY OLD GRIEFS, AND WITH MY CHILDHOOD'S FAITH.

I LOVE THEE

WITH A LOVE

I SEEMED TO LOSE

WITH MY LOST SAINTS—

I LOVE THEE WITH THE BREATH, SMILES, TEARS, OF ALL MY LIFE!—

AND, IF GOD CHOOSE,

I SHALL BUT LOVE THEE BETTER AFTER DEATH.

END

The Rubáiyát

of Omar Khayyám

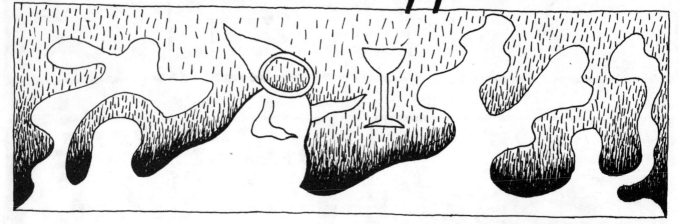

of Naishápúr

Translated by Edward FitzGerald

1.   Wake! For the Sun, who scattered into flight
      The Stars before him from the Field of Night,
         Drives Night along with them from Heav'n, and strikes
      The Sultan's Turret with a Shaft of Light.

7.   Come, fill the Cup, and in the fire of Spring
      Your Winter-garment of Repentence fling:
         The Bird of Time has but a little way
      To flutter — and the Bird is on the Wing.

12.   A Book of Verses underneath the Bough,
       A Jug of Wine, a Loaf of Bread — and Thou
         Beside me singing in the Wilderness —
       Oh, Wilderness were Paradise enow !

27.   Myself when young did eagerly frequent
       Doctor and Saint, and heard great argument
         About it and about: but evermore
       Came out by the same door where in I went.

43.   So when that Angel of the darker Drink
        At last shall find you by the river-brink,
           And, offering his Cup, invite your Soul
        Forth to your Lips to quaff — you shall not shrink.

55.   You know, my Friends, with what a brave Carouse
        I made a Second Marriage in my house;
           Divorced old barren Reason from my Bed,
        And took the Daughter of the Vine to Spouse.

68.　We are no other than a moving row
　　　Of Magic Shadow-shapes that come and go
　　　　Round with the *Sun*-illumined Lantern held
　　　In Midnight by the Master of the Show;

69.　But helpless Pieces of the Game He plays
　　　Upon his Checkerboard of Nights and Days;
　　　　Hither and thither moves, and checks, and slays,
　　　And one by one back in the Closet lays.

End

THE EAGLE

HE CLASPS THE CRAG WITH CROOKED HANDS:

BY ALFRED, LORD TENNYSON

CLOSE TO THE SUN IN LONELY LANDS,

RINGED WITH THE AZURE WORLD, HE STANDS.

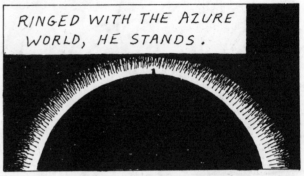

THE WRINKLED SEA BENEATH HIM CRAWLS;

HE WATCHES FROM HIS MOUNTAIN WALLS,

AND LIKE

A THUNDERBOLT

HE

FALLS.

END

AND THE STATELY SHIPS GO ON

TO THEIR HAVEN UNDER THE HILL;

BUT O FOR THE TOUCH OF A VANISHED HAND

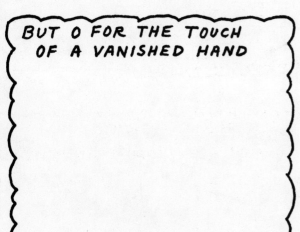

AND THE SOUND OF A VOICE THAT IS STILL!

BREAK, BREAK, BREAK,
   AT THE FOOT OF THY CRAGS, O SEA!
BUT THE TENDER GRACE OF A DAY THAT IS
   DEAD
      WILL NEVER COME BACK TO ME.

END

"THE WOODS DECAY, THE WOODS DECAY AND FALL,
THE VAPORS WEEP THEIR BURTHEN TO THE GROUND,
MAN COMES AND TILLS THE FIELD AND LIES BENEATH,
AND AFTER MANY A SUMMER DIES THE SWAN."

ALFRED, LORD TENNYSON

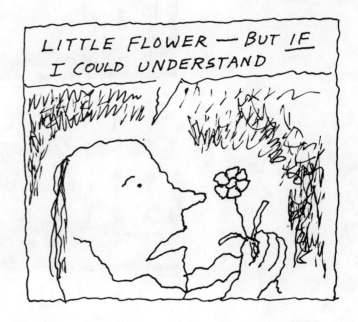

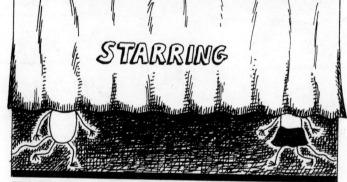

109

END

"THAT'S MY LAST DUCHESS PAINTED
ON THE WALL, LOOKING AS IF
SHE WERE ALIVE."

ROBERT BROWNING

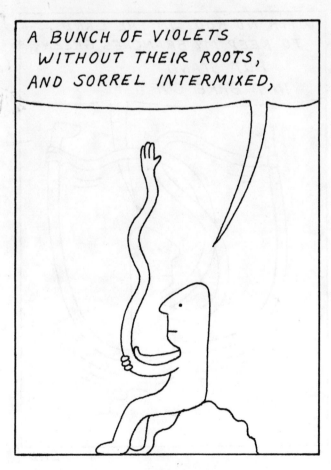

A NOSEGAY WHICH TIME
CLUTCHED FROM OUT
THOSE FAIR ELYSIAN FIELDS,

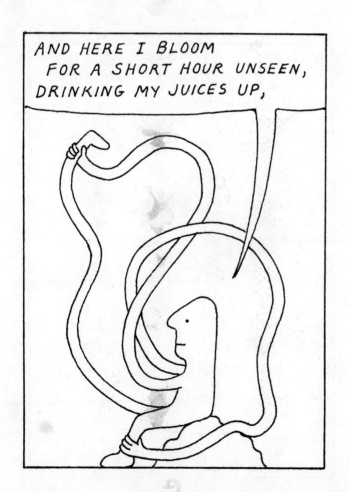

WITH WEEDS AND BROKEN STEMS,
IN HASTE,
DOTH MAKE THE RABBLE ROUT
THAT WASTE
THE DAY HE YIELDS.

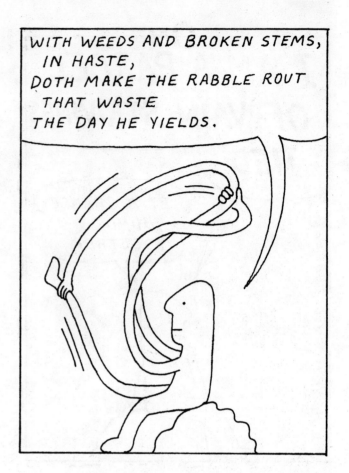

AND HERE I BLOOM
FOR A SHORT HOUR UNSEEN,
DRINKING MY JUICES UP,

WITH NO ROOT IN THE LAND
TO KEEP MY BRANCHES GREEN,
BUT STAND
IN A BARE CUP.

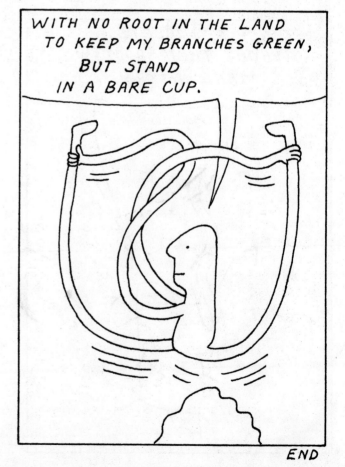

END

ONE'S-SELF I SING

BY WALT WHITMAN

ONE'S-SELF I SING, A SIMPLE SEPARATE PERSON,

YET UTTER THE WORD DEMOCRATIC,

THE WORD EN-MASSE.

OF PHYSIOLOGY FROM TOP TO TOE I SING,

NOT PHYSIOGNOMY ALONE, NOR BRAIN ALONE

IS WORTHY FOR THE MUSE,

I SAY THE FORM COMPLETE IS WORTHIER FAR,

THE FEMALE EQUALLY WITH THE MALE I SING.

OF LIFE IMMENSE IN PASSION, PULSE, AND POWER,

CHEERFUL, FOR FREEST ACTION

FORM'D UNDER THE LAWS DIVINE,

THE MODERN MAN I SING.

THE ADVENTURES OF WHITMAN

IT'S A BARD... IT'S A POET... IT'S...

— WORDS FROM "LEAVES OF GRASS" —

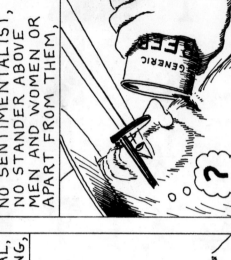

WALT WHITMAN, A KOSMOS, OF MANHATTAN, THE SON,

TURBULENT, FLESHY, SENSUAL, EATING, DRINKING AND BREEDING,

NO SENTIMENTALIST, NO STANDER ABOVE MEN AND WOMEN OR APART FROM THEM,

FROM PAUMANOK STARTING I FLY LIKE A BIRD,

UNSCREW THE LOCKS FROM THEIR DOORS! UNSCREW THE DOORS THEMSELVES FROM THEIR JAMBS!

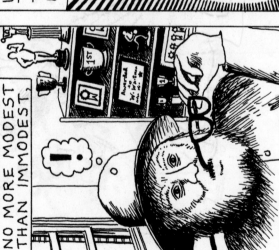

NO MORE MODEST THAN IMMODEST,

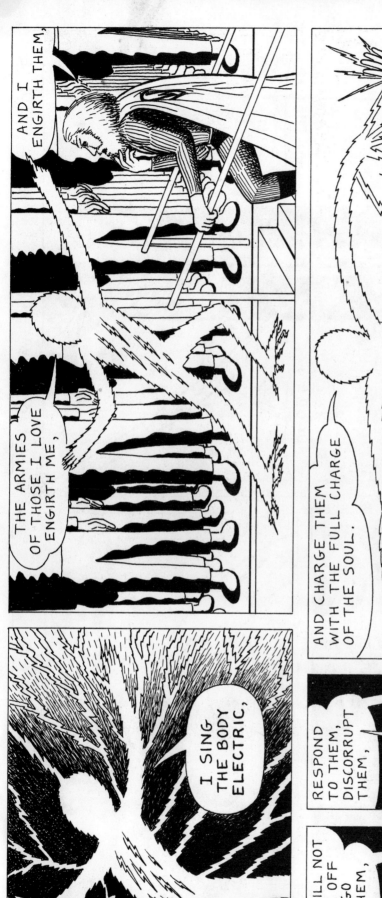
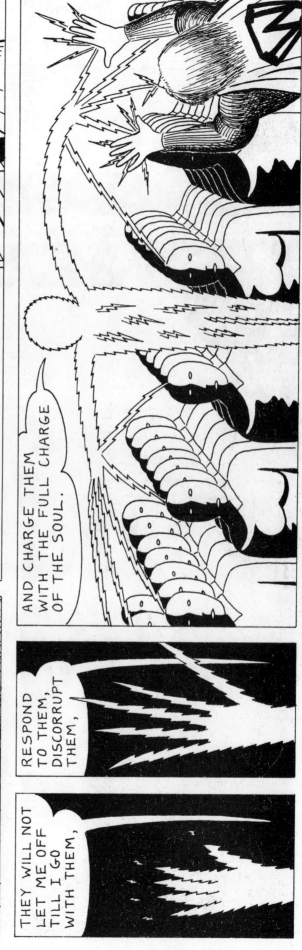

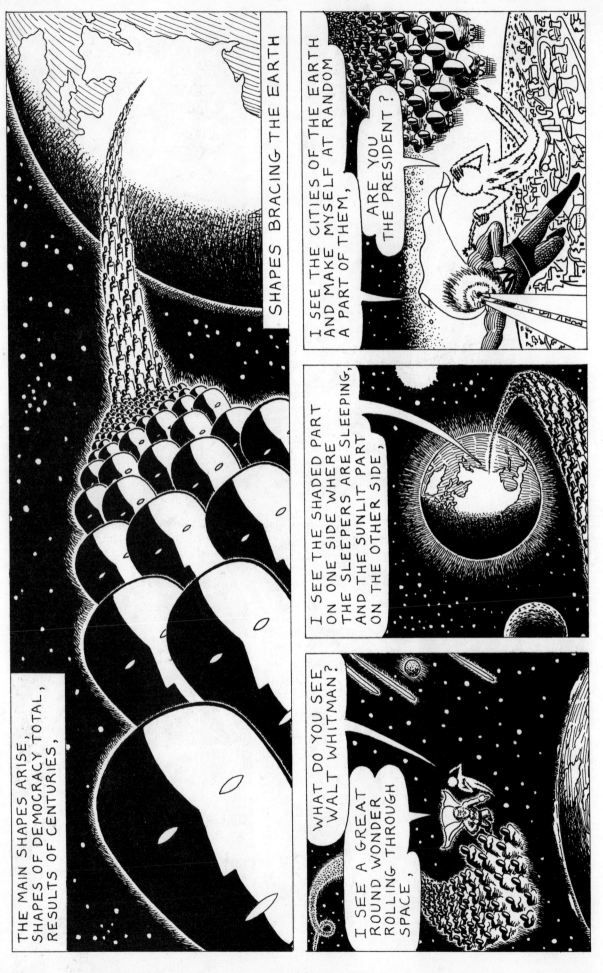

END

123

712

BY EMILY DICKINSON

BECAUSE I COULD NOT STOP FOR DEATH,

HE KINDLY STOPPED FOR ME;

DEATH

712

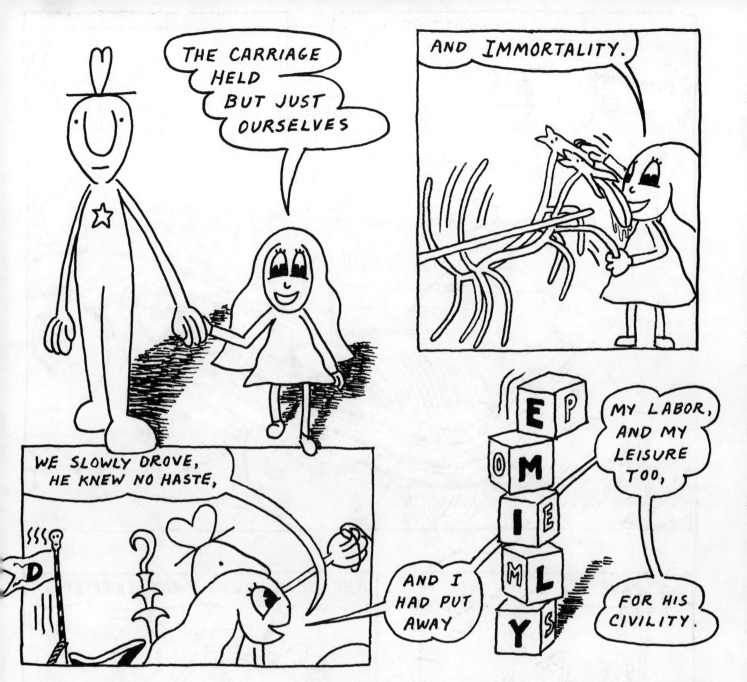

" I CANNOT LIVE WITH YOU,   IT WOULD BE LIFE,
AND LIFE IS OVER THERE   BEHIND THE SHELF "

EMILY DICKINSON

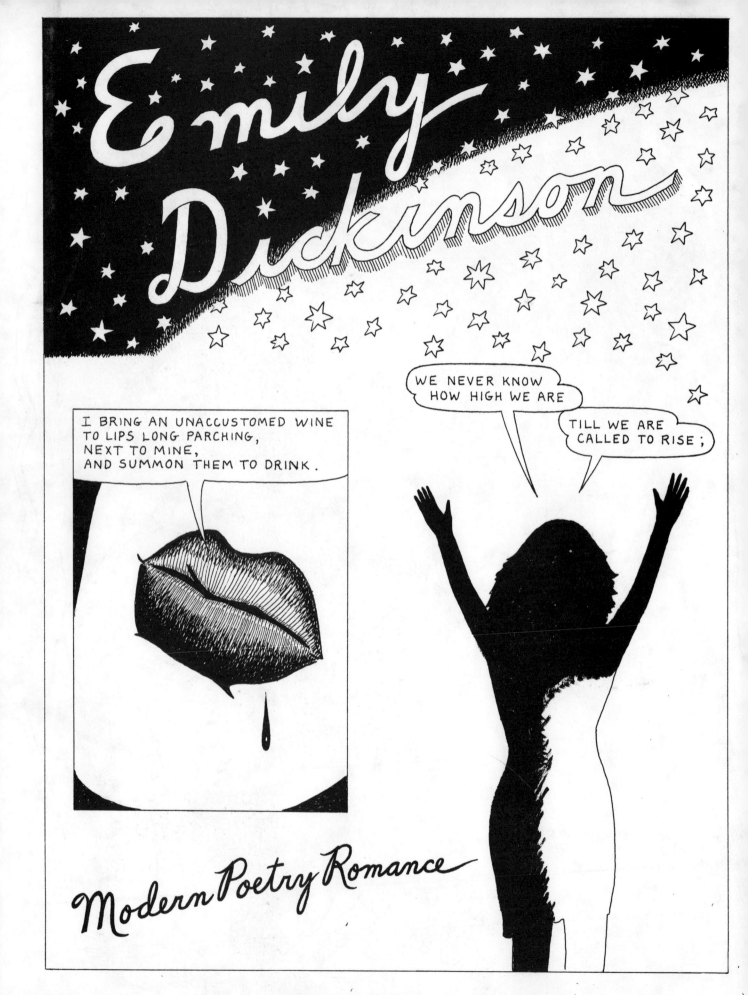

END

JABBERWOCKY

BY LEWIS CARROLL

'TWAS BRILLIG, AND THE SLITHY TOVES DID GYRE AND GIMBLE IN THE WABE:

ALL MIMSY WERE THE BOROGOVES, AND THE MOME RATHS OUTGRABE.

"BEWARE THE JABBERWOCK, MY SON! THE JAWS THAT BITE, THE CLAWS THAT CATCH. BEWARE THE JUBJUB BIRD, AND SHUN THE FRUMIOUS BANDERSNATCH!"

HE TOOK HIS VORPAL SWORD IN HAND; LONG TIME THE MANXOME FOE HE SOUGHT— SO RESTED HE BY THE TUMTUM TREE, AND STOOD AWHILE IN THOUGHT.

CHECKERBOARD

ON THE HORIZON

by STEPHEN CRANE

On the horizon, the peaks assembled;

And as I looked,

The march of the mountains began.

As they marched, they sang,

"Ay! We come! We come!"

END

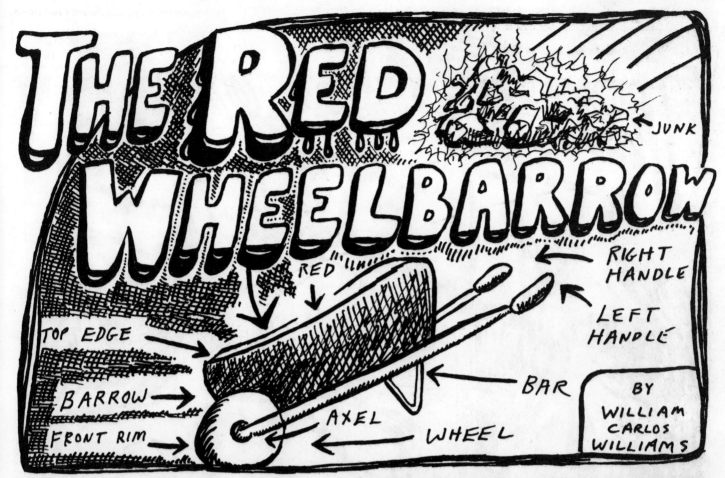

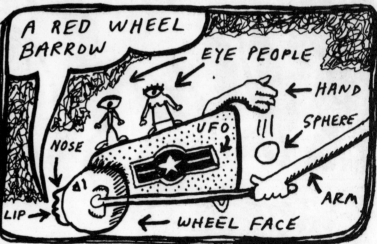

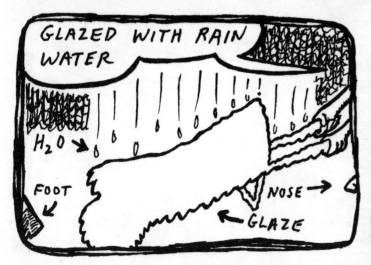

END

NO EYES OR EARS LEFT

TO DO THEIR OWN DOINGS

(ALL

INVADED, APPROPRIATED, OUTRAGED,

ALL SENSES

INCLUDING

THE MIND,

THAT WORKER ON WHAT IS

AND THAT OTHER SENSE

MADE

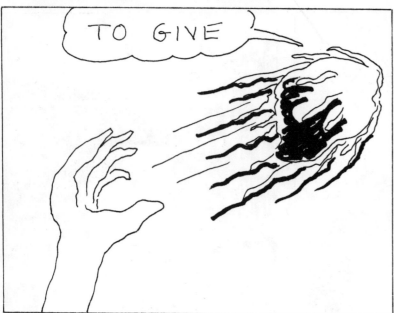

TO GIVE

EVEN THE MOST WRETCHED

OR ANY OF US,

WRETCHED,

END

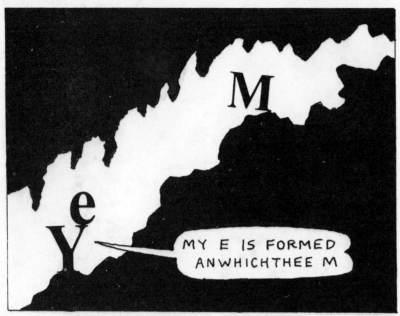

147

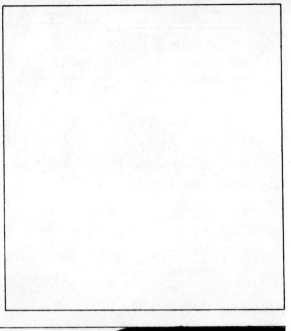

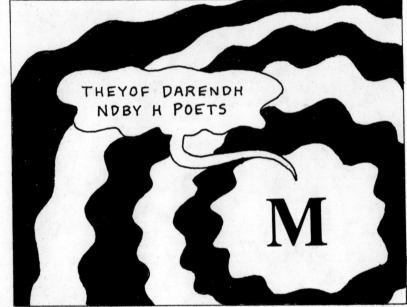

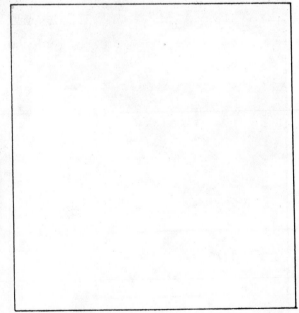

END

END

"HOLD BACK THE EDGES OF YOUR GOWNS, LADIES, WE ARE GOING THROUGH HELL." —W.C. WILLIAMS

BY ALLEN GINSBERG

HOWL

FOR CARL SOLOMON

I SAW THE BEST MINDS OF MY GENERATION DESTROYED BY MADNESS,

STARVING HYSTERICAL NAKED,

DRAGGING THEMSELVES THROUGH THE NEGRO STREETS AT DAWN

LOOKING FOR AN ANGRY FIX,

ANGELHEADED HIPSTERS BURNING FOR THE ANCIENT HEAVENLY CONNECTION TO THE STARRY DYNAMO

IN THE MACHINERY OF NIGHT,

WHO POVERTY AND TATTERS AND HOLLOW-EYED AND HIGH SAT UP SMOKING IN THE SUPERNATURAL DARKNESS OF COLD-WATER FLATS FLOATING ACROSS THE TOPS OF CITIES CONTEMPLATING

JAZZ,

WHO BARED THEIR BRAINS TO HEAVEN UNDER THE EL AND SAW

MOHAMMEDAN ANGELS STAGGERING ON TENEMENT ROOFS ILLUMINATED,

WHO PASSED THROUGH UNIVERSITIES WITH RADIANT COOL EYES HALLUCINATING ARKANSAS AND BLAKE-LIGHT TRAGEDY

AMONG THE SCHOLARS OF WAR,

WHO WERE EXPELLED FROM THE ACADEMIES FOR CRAZY

AND PUBLISHING OBSCENE ODES ON THE WINDOWS OF THE SKULL,

WHO COWERED IN UNSHAVEN ROOMS IN UNDERWEAR,

BURNING THEIR MONEY IN WASTEBASKETS

MONOPOLY

AND LISTENING TO THE TERROR THROUGH THE WALL,

WHO GOT BUSTED IN THEIR PUBIC BEARDS RETURNING THROUGH LAREDO WITH A BELT OF MARIJUANA FOR NEW YORK,

WHO ATE FIRE IN PAINT HOTELS

OR DRANK TURPENTINE IN PARADISE ALLEY, DEATH,

OR PURGATORIED THEIR TORSOS NIGHT AFTER NIGHT WITH DREAMS, WITH DRUGS, WITH WAKING NIGHTMARES, ALCOHOL AND COCK AND ENDLESS BALLS,

INCOMPARABLE BLIND STREETS
OF SHUDDERING CLOUD
AND LIGHTNING IN THE MIND
LEAPING TOWARD POLES
OF CANADA AND PATERSON,

ILLUMINATING

ALL THE MOTIONLESS WORLD

OF TIME BETWEEN,

PEYOTE SOLIDITIES OF HALLS,
BACKYARD GREEN TREE
CEMETERY DAWNS, WINE
DRUNKENNESS OVER
THE ROOFTOPS, STOREFRONT
BOROUGHS OF TEAHEAD
JOYRIDE NEON BLINKING
TRAFFIC LIGHT, SUN AND
MOON AND TREE VIBRATIONS
IN THE ROARING WINTER
DUSKS OF BROOKLYN,

ASHCAN RANTINGS

AND

KIND KING LIGHT OF MIND,

WHO CHAINED THEMSELVES
TO SUBWAYS FOR THE ENDLESS
RIDE FROM BATTERY TO
HOLY BRONX ON BENZEDRINE

UNTIL THE NOISE OF WHEELS
AND CHILDREN BROUGHT THEM DOWN
SHUDDERING MOUTH-WRACKED
AND BATTERED BLEAK OF BRAIN

ALL DRAINED
OF BRILLIANCE
IN THE DREAR LIGHT
OF ZOO,

WHO SANK ALL NIGHT IN SUBMARINE LIGHT OF BICKFORD'S

FLOATED OUT AND

SAT THROUGH THE STALE BEER AFTERNOON IN DESOLATE FUGAZZI'S,

LISTENING TO THE CRACK OF DOOM ON THE HYDROGEN JUKEBOX,

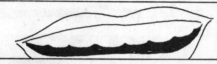

WHO TALKED CONTINUOUSLY SEVENTY HOURS FROM PARK TO PAD TO BAR TO BELLEVUE TO MUSEUM TO THE BROOKLYN BRIDGE,

DAILY NEWS

A LOST BATTALION OF PLATONIC CONVERSATIONALISTS

JUMPING DOWN THE STOOPS OFF FIRE ESCAPES OFF WINDOWSILLS OFF EMPIRE STATE OUT OF THE MOON,

YACKETAYAKKING SCREAMING VOMITING WHISPERING FACTS AND MEMORIES AND ANECDOTES AND EYEBALL KICKS AND SHOCKS OF HOSPITALS AND JAILS AND WARS,

162

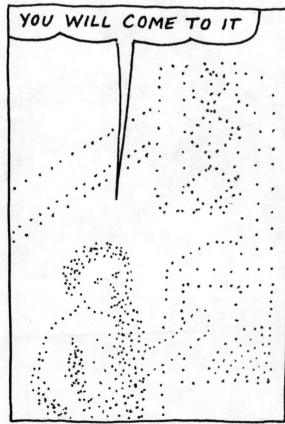

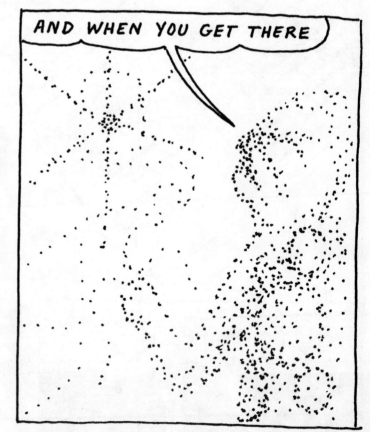

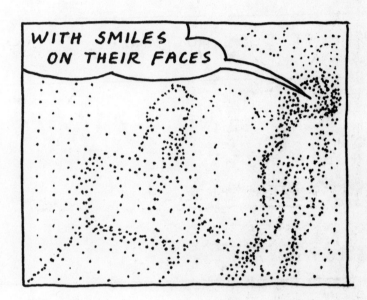

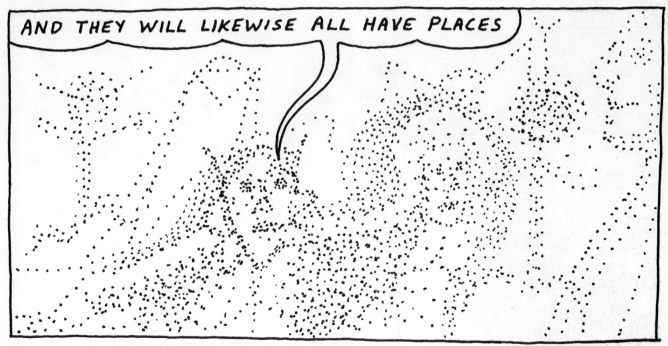

END

THE CORNER

BY DONALD HALL

IT DOES NOT KNOW   ITS NAME.

IT SITS   IN A DAMP CORNER,

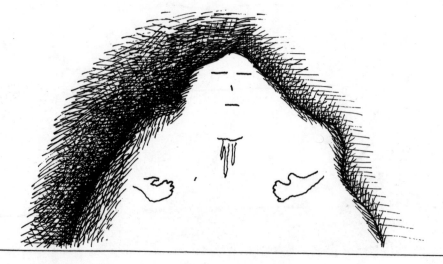

SPIT HANGING   FROM ITS CHIN,

ODOR OF URINE   PUDDLED AROUND.

HUGE, HAIRLESS, GRUNTING,   IT PLAYS WITH ITSELF,

SLEEPS,

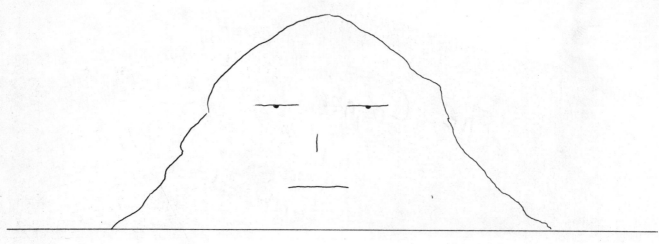

STARES FOR HOURS,

AND LEAPS

TO SMASH ITSELF ON THE WALL.

LIMPING, BLOODY,

FALLING BACK   INTO THE CORNER,

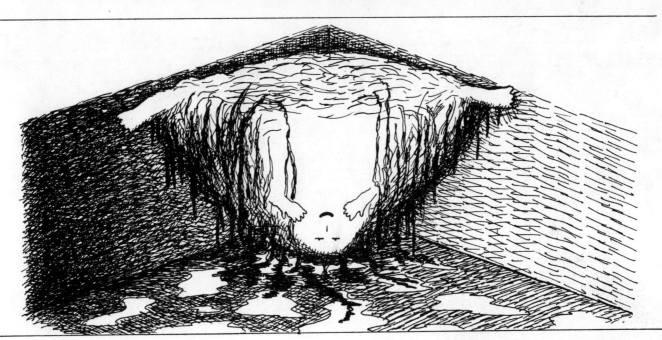

IT WILL NOT DIE.   END

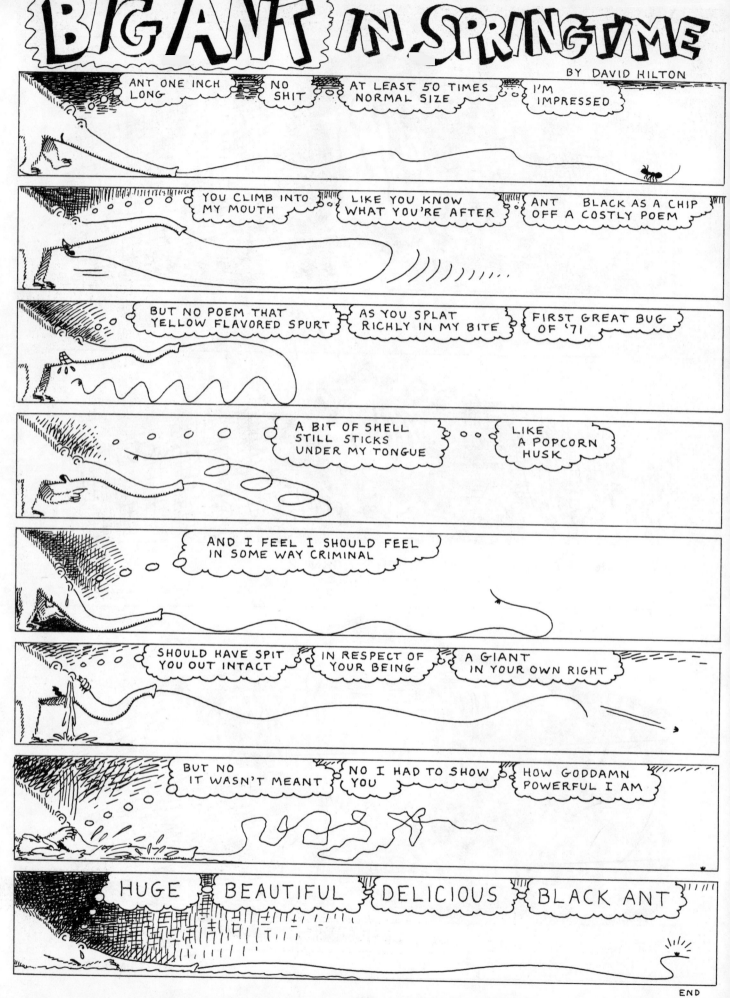

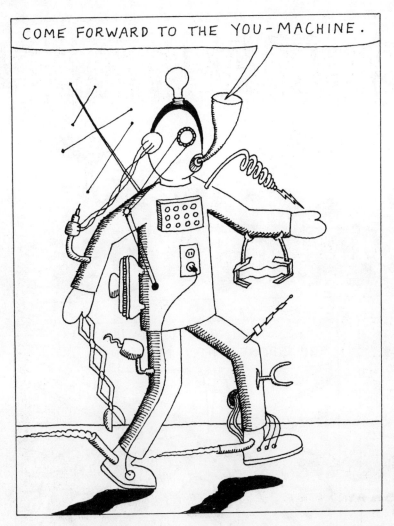

COME FORWARD TO THE YOU-MACHINE.

THE EYE MACHINE

RECORDS THE MIST MACHINES

ENTANGLED IN THE TREE MACHINES,

RELEASING TWIG MACHINE BY TWIG MACHINE

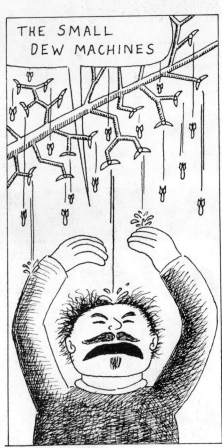

THE SMALL DEW MACHINES

WHILE IN THE HOUSE MACHINES

THE PEOPLE MACHINES

SLIP INTO THE SLEEP MACHINES,

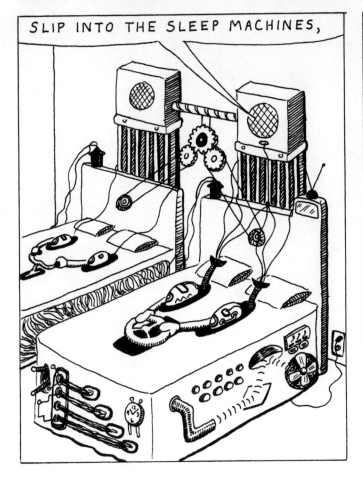

THEIR LOVE MACHINES SILENTLY RUNNING.

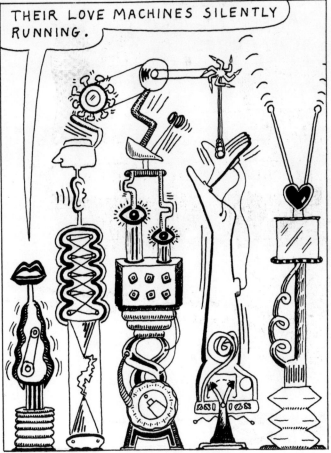

END

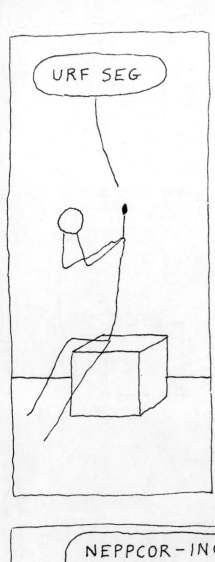
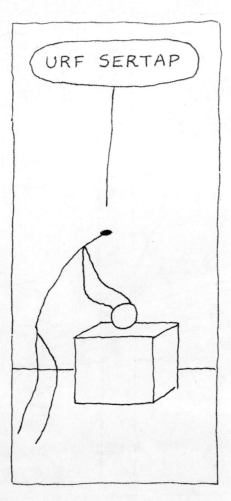
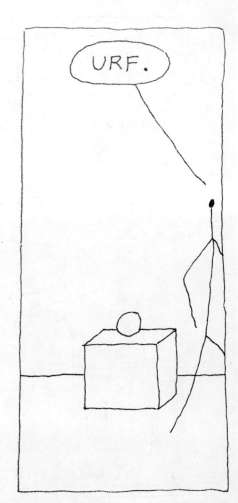

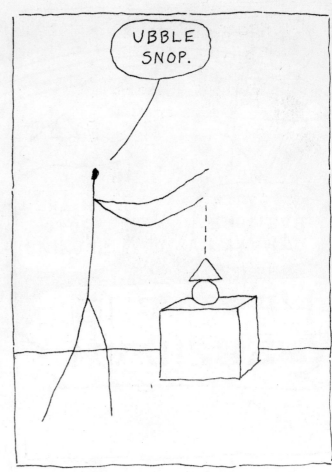

END

END

SCHEDULE SE
(Form 1040)
Department of the Treasury
Internal Revenue Service

Computation of Social Security Poem ◄ ◄ ◄
► See Instructions for Schedule SE (Form 1040).
► Attach to Form 1040.

1981

23

Name of self-employed person (as shown on social security card)	Social security number of self-employed person ►		

Your social security number determines your own unique poem hidden in a billion possible poems below. To find yours, just circle the nine digits of your social security number, one digit per column. Begin with the A-column for your first digit, and continue through I. The corresponding phrases, when read in the order of their selection, form your nine-line 1981 Social Security Poem. Not only is it free verse, it's tax-deductible!

A
1. As the wheels
2. When other planets
3. Because her acorns
4. Since your lips
5. While those mannikins
6. If these shadows
7. After his dogs
8. Although our trucks
9. Before both dancers
0. Until their faces

B
1. were sleeping on
2. are flying around
3. don't bother
4. laughed at
5. bounced off
6. march around
7. will stumble over
8. can't taste
9. might paint
0. won't speak to

C
1. the singer's mouth,
2. his antique television,
3. her grand piano player,
4. these sad sandwiches,
5. those beautiful blue teeth,
6. that mindless table,
7. this magic Buick,
8. their golden typewriters,
9. an optical illusion,
0. a missing link,

D
1. he tried to whistle
2. she slapped him
3. he saw a ghost
4. she always grinned
5. he chuckled once
6. she wished him luck
7. he just pushed buttons
8. she read minds
9. he never sneezed
0. she almost ate dinner

E
1. down the sink.
2. against their beliefs.
3. between two mirrors.
4. at the Crystal Café.
5. like her telephone.
6. with the devil's lighter.
7. across Kansas.
8. without starlight.
9. in his dream.
0. out of sheer desire.

F
1. Her modern poetry
2. His astral projection
3. These lightning bolts
4. Their bathtub gin
5. That parking ramp
6. Random numbers
7. Your gothic romance
8. Those laser beams
9. My green thumb
0. The space shuttle

G
1. awkwardly
2. silently
3. jealously
4. haphazardly
5. neatly
6. voraciously
7. pitifully
8. gleefully
9. frankly
0. longingly

H
1. frightened the gnomes
2. pulled the plug
3. stunned the barber
4. praised the clock
5. attracted the mice
6. troubled the professor
7. boiled the shapes
8. angered the ambassador
9. caught the butterfly
0. bewildered the muse

I
1. floating in my soup.
2. upholstering his lawn.
3. naming those plants.
4. watching like an elephant.
5. looking for Fred.
6. training her cat.
7. evicting the landlord.
8. burning your toast.
9. hiding in their cellar.
0. glowing like a lamp.

The
Poetry
Handbook

The lunatic, the lover, and the poet
Are of imagination all compact ;

William Shakespeare

May I a small house, and large garden have!

Abraham Cowley

Lo! sweeten'd with the summer light,
The full-juiced apple, waxing over-mellow,

Alfred, Lord Tennyson

I am out of humanity's reach,
I must finish my journey alone,

William Cowper

Once again
Do I behold these steep and lofty cliffs,

William Wordsworth

All love, all liking, all delight
Lies drowned with us in endless night.

Robert Herrick

Goe and catch a falling star,

John Donne

End

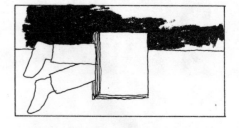